A Booklet for Hotel Managers and Others

I0472923

7

EASY Ways to Show Your Employees YOU Care!

Jokima Hiller

outskirtspress

DENVER, COLORADO

Dedicated to
all managers who strive to make a difference
in the work lives of their team

Contents

Foreword i

Introduction..v

Way 1: 10 Minutes of Happiness 1

Way 2: Celebrate ME..3

Way 3: The Word-on-the-Streets 5

Way 4: A Hospitality Welcome................................8

Way 5: SMILE!..10

Way 6: Just Be You...12

Way 7: Break Bread – OFTEN................................14

Caring Ways Enhance the Circle of Life

      for any Business...16

About the Author...19

Testimonials...21

Foreword

THE ESSENCE OF hospitality is measured by relationships . . . relationships with co-workers, relationships with owners, relationships with associates, relationships with guests, and even relationships with competitors. However, the manager/associate relationship is at the very core of the essence. This booklet and these ways for showing your associates that you care foster the beginning of a relationship built upon trust.

I remember the beginning of my relationship with Jokima Hiller. She was referred to me by a friend, Teresa Torres. Teresa was the Executive Director of Everybody Counts. She asked me to give this young high school student a chance. There sitting across from me at our very first meeting was a very shy 15 year old young lady. Jokima wouldn't even lift her head during our meetings let alone make eye contact. So I let her know that if she didn't look me in the eyes I would stop talking to her! From that day forward, Jokima made progress in overcoming her shyness. She lifted her head, looked at me, and we began to build a working relationship based upon trust that would turn into a lifelong friendship.

At the time, I was the Director of Human Resources of a full service hotel and she was an intern. When I asked her to complete a task, she did so and always exceeded my expectations. I've witnessed her journey and today she's offering a booklet with ideas that are simple and direct, easy to understand and talk about, as well as put to use in the workplace. Individually, each of the seven (7) ways to care for your associates is a good conversation piece that creates an ongoing dialogue with your associates. She has presented these ways to care at the- foot-on-the-ground everyday basic level.

What is most special about this booklet is that the topic of caring for people transcends cultural, racial, language, and other barriers to relationships. The outcome is that people's performance will be enhanced and reinforce that they belong to something larger than themselves. There is a good amount of fortune generated by each of these seven ways, not because of the lucky number 7 but because they allow supervisors to foster a relationship with their team in a heartfelt way.

In a fashion, the seven ways to care mirror Jokima's performance at our hotel. As front desk manager, she would deliver her Associate of the Month (AOM) nominations at the AOM recognition luncheon as if it was a testimonial of the associate's performance and character. Her nomination would provide detailed and specific examples of how her nominee contributed to the success of the department and was therefore worthy of the award. You just sensed that everybody

in the room wanted to feel what her associate felt –
cared for and greatly appreciated by her manager.
Further, many of those managers and associates se-
cretly wished that she was their manager too. I've never again seen anyone else do this better than Jokima.
Thank you for the privilege of writing the Foreword to
your book.

John Szczepanski
Senior Director of Associate Relations and Risk Management
White Lodging Services - 30 Years of Service

Introduction

According to a Gallup poll, feeling unappreciated is the number one reason why employees leave their jobs.

WHEN I STARTED in the hospitality industry, working at a hotel, I worked in the human resources department. I was a teenager and was shocked by the number of "problems" managers had with their employees. Fast forward 20 years and while I no longer work in human resources, I interact with hospitality students, graduates, and professionals in the industry and guess what? Managers continue to have employee issues. I listen intently to the stories and as simple as it sounds, "My boss doesn't care about me." seems to be the root of many employer problems. Connecting with employees can easily reduce problems and build employee appreciation for you and what your organization offers.

Yes, benefits, salary, and physical working conditions could all be in alignment with an employee's expectations, but, how you make them feel is what they remember for years to come. Did you say "thank you" for a job well done, smile or empathize with them on a day when things just weren't going right? Caring for someone is an action . . . as a manager, you must put in some effort to connect with your team to exhibit your thoughtfulness, concern, and compassion. You may feel thoughtfulness, concern and compassion in your heart for your team; however, they can't see what's there or know what you think or how you feel. You must show them.

I know you're busy, so I won't take much of your time. In the next few pages, I'll outline 7 <u>easy</u> ways to actively show your team that you care. I have tried MANY ways to show my employees that I care – some have failed miserably while others have been successful in helping me develop a positive working relationship with my team. The ideas offered in this booklet have been used by me in my employment history and I am excited to share them with you!

Way 1: 10 Minutes of Happiness

I realized that I couldn't prevent my team from walking into a situation that would most likely lead to them having a bad day. Imagine, for example, a hotel housekeeper with 12 rooms to clean for the day walking into a room that has been trashed by the guest. This, for most housekeepers, is the beginning of an awful day.

I WANTED TO insulate my team so that when they encountered a challenging situation, such as a trashed room, they were prepared. The insulation process included making the back office area of the business a 10 minute happy and cheerful place to be.

Employees would arrive at work and right above the time clock was the joke of the day. They could get a cup of coffee with a variety of cream options just like their guests. Employees could sit, and in a relaxing environment, look at exciting and engaging bulletin boards full of employee recognition, highlights of departmental successes, and positive guest comments.

When you set up your 10 Minutes of Happiness environment, make sure you choose a spot where all employees will feel comfortable going to. This could be a break room or some sort of back office area out of site of the public. This is your opportunity to show your staff not only that you care but that you care about them just as much as you care about your customers. It only takes a little bit of effort to choose a joke of the day or even of the week. It only takes a little bit of effort to decorate a designated bulletin board or walls. It only takes a little bit of effort to provide coffee or a beverage that your employees will enjoy.

The goal here is to provide employees with 10 minutes of happiness before they report to their duties as assigned. I would tell my team that "I can't guarantee what happens once you step outside of these back office doors, but I hope you feel good enough to handle *whatever* you encounter!" This is just one simple way to show your employees you care.

Way 2: Celebrate ME

"Team awards are great Ms. Jokima, but I did this and I did that. . ." In hearing this more than a few times, I recognized that employees want to be looked at as individuals who make up the team.

MY EMPLOYEES, IN their own way, were screaming "Celebrate ME!" It's true that teamwork is essential and necessary for most businesses to operate effectively; however, we must also create opportunities that value the individuals and the job they do as members of the team. This could mean an employee of the month program, an employee spotlight in the monthly employee newsletter, or any other variety of programs that brings recognition to your staff. Just make sure it is all about the individual employee and who they are as a person.

In order to get your Celebrate ME program up and running, be sure to ask your staff for their input. Do they want to celebrate birthdays or work anniversaries? Are they interested in something monthly or yearly or would they prefer to be "surprised?" For example, what's their favorite color, favorite snack, favorite candy bar, and favorite beverage? When the Celebrate ME moment arrives, place their favorite items into their favorite colored gift bag with colored tissue paper. Yes, it sounds simple, and it is!

The goal here is to provide employees with something just for them, all for them, and include things only they like and appreciate. You'd be amazed at how many times I heard employees say "This is just for me?" or "Oh wow, this is my favorite color!" Be sure to take a picture of them and their gift bag to add to your 10 Minutes of Happiness bulletin board! Show that you care by celebrating the `ME' in all employees and the job they do for your business.

Way 3: The Word-on-the-Streets

"What? Who doesn't like who?" I found out that two of my associates were feuding right under my nose, and I was clueless! That one situation made me understand the employee/supervisor dynamic. Because of fear of negative consequences, employees are NOT going to tell you what's going on in your own department or company.

I REMEMBER THE day just like it was yesterday, I humbly asked my staff what could I do to be "in the know?" I wanted to help them have an enjoyable time on their jobs, but I couldn't achieve this if I didn't know what was wrong and how to fix it. I am a big proponent of "one-on-ones" where you get a chance to check-in with your staff and find out what's working and what's not working. But, in some instances, even these types of meetings are fruitless because employees feel that they'll be penalized for bringing up something negative. This barrier must be removed. The grapevine is alive and well in most businesses and here are two things to note: 1) Managers aren't included in this grapevine and 2) Much of what is talked about in the grapevine is rooted in truth.

My employees, that I posed the question to, were mostly young males and they responded saying they wanted to be able to trust me. They said, "We want to be able to trust you when we tell you what the word is on the streets and that you won't write us up or terminate us."

I deeply thought about what they were asking and offered this. . ."I will give you all a grace moment where you can share with me any and everything without judgment or repercussions. I will follow-up on only those items that I can control and will promise to not implicate you. If we are dealing with something that is illegal or harmful, I will work WITH you to resolve it." My conversation with this group would begin with "Hey guys, so what's the word-on-the-streets today?" It is such a simple question, yet it yielded quite complex answers that helped me to 1) better connect with my employees, 2) build trust where in most employer/ supervisor relationships there is none, and 3) become aware of issues that we were able to resolve together. During this time, I formed a bond with my hotel bellmen and shuttle drivers that afforded us conversations and experiences that can never be duplicated. I showed them that I cared and they rewarded me with their trust. Trust was the goal.

Through the word-on-the-streets process I was able to get assistance for a shuttle driver who had an alcohol problem. Through the-word-on-the-streets process I was able to facilitate an environment that when two associates weren't getting along they were able to work it out. Through the word-on-the-streets I was told about non-functioning equipment, guest complaints, and problems in other departments that I was able to address at management meetings. Make showing that you care the new Word-on-the-Streets among your team.

Way 4: A Hospitality Welcome

Everyone remembers when they were the "new guy!" My siblings and I have oftentimes joked about being new students in a big school and not being able to find our classes, the restroom, or the cafeteria. No mother wants to hear that her child hasn't eaten all week because he or she didn't find the lunchroom! Well, no new employee wants to feel as lost and out-of-place.

MY COLLEAGUES TEASE me saying that I go overboard in this area, but the truth is I just want to give my new employee a good, exciting, and welcoming start. This means that I may just do any of the following on his or her first day to create a sense of belonging:

- Buy flowers
- Take them to lunch
- Provide a gift bag of snacks and goodies
- Orient and train them myself
- Greet them at the door
- Give them a guided tour
- Introduce them to the team
- A handwritten note
- Have a welcome reception

- Personally bring them a cup of coffee or something to drink

There are a few things that I will do for ALL new employees and that is make sure they have a name-tag, uniform (if applicable), a clean work area (desk, housekeeping cart, office, etc.), and knowledge of where the restrooms are located.

The goal is to truly make the new guy feel welcome on their new job. This sets the tone for their employment and may be the first opportunity you have to show your employee that you care. Keep it simple – if giving flowers aren't in your budget, buy one flower and place it in a cup with water on their desk. A handwritten note with the words "Glad to have you on the team!" can go a long way. Just taking time out of your schedule to be the tour guide on their first day can help paint the picture that you are a supervisor that cares. A hospitable welcome helps new employees experience your own brand of hospitality and care.

Way 5: SMILE!

Just like the pineapple, a smile is a symbol of hospitality service.

IN ANY SERVICE related industry, the smile is a part of the uniform. We are trained to put our smiles on for every guest interaction. The guest may be having a bad day and a smile is what we offer to brighten their day. In the hotel industry particularly, we talk about how the tired traveler who's been through so much to make it to our property deserves our kindness delivered with a smile and welcome greeting. On the contrary, who smiles at the employee?

If you are fortunate enough to have a team of hardworking employees, a smile is the least you could offer them every day. If your team is not hardworking, a smile should still be offered. Until you walk in their shoes (just like the traveler) and know what they've been through to get here, a smile should be given to each associate. Just by turning up the sides of your mouth, you can uplift a bad mood, encourage someone, build trust, and be friendly.

The goal is for you to extend the olive branch, a peace offering, and to show yourself friendly. Your smile may encourage that less than hardworking employee to pull their weight or may warm the heart of an employee that is living a hard and difficult life outside of work. Your smile helps set the tone for a welcoming and positive work environment. As the leader, your team looks to you for guidance and will mirror your mood and countenance. When I used to interview hospitality candidates I looked for a smile in the interview. I actually passed on a bell staff applicant who didn't smile once in the interview process. Likewise, the interviewee is looking for that same gesture of hospitality. It puts them at ease and gives them a preview of how you'll relate to them on the job. May your smile be your personal way to show you care.

Way 6: Just Be You

Every 'fix my business' show you see on television, where the owners are struggling, usually includes a conversation with the staff. The "fixer" finds out that the team, based on perception, had no clue of how bad things were financially for the business.

CLEARLY, THERE IS a disconnect. This sort of disconnect breeds distrust of managers and owners. Employees think the organization's leaders are making lots of money and not sharing it with the staff. Sometimes employees even look at their supervisors as cold, inhumane, and unreal. Early on in my career, the word "stoic" seemed to follow me around. My employees thought I never had a bad day, was never affected by guest issues, and could handle anything. Boy, were they wrong!

It is ok for your team to see a different side of who you are – a vulnerable side impacted by the ups and downs of the daily operations. No, I'm not saying get all soft-like and hold crying sessions, but be willing to just be you. Share what's going on and how you feel about it. If the business is failing, your team needs to know that and you may have to humble yourself to share that information. Or, if you lose a loved one, let them know how bad it hurts. Likewise, if something fabulous happens, be willing to be excited! The goal is to show your team that you are a real person with feelings and capable of caring for others. I think the kids today say it best – "Keep it 100!" Keep it 100 for a Just Being You – YOU.

Way 7: Break Bread — OFTEN

Whether you prepare it with your own hands or buy it, eating a meal together is a common language that crosses many bridges and can bind many teams.

IN THE HOSPITALITY industry, specifically hotels, taking time to eat was a rarity. You were usually on-the-go for most of your shift, and when you did eat, you were most likely alone in the break room or in your office. By this time, the food was cold. You ate quick praying that you didn't drop anything on your uniform as you'd surely be interrupted and need to help out at the front desk or in a guest area. My mother used to leave me voicemail messages urging me to remember to eat something and well, to take a restroom break. The latter is another day's story, but, today let's focus on the caring nature of sharing a meal with someone.

I promised myself that once I was in a position in my career where I could take a lunch, I would AND I would share that time with my team. I doubt that you think about breaking bread with your staff; however, you do think about spending time with friends and family and food is at the center of that thought. With family and friends, we eat to celebrate birthdays, anniversaries, holidays, and even lives at a funeral repast. Being at the table with others can be honorable, intimate, celebratory, but more importantly special. This is the goal to show your team that they are special enough for you to take time out of your busy schedule to eat along with them. For this way to show you care to truly be beneficial, don't just buy lunch for everyone. You need to sit down with them and eat. I've learned so much about my employees during this time as they were more at ease. Who can be upset when consuming good food? No one. Right!

Just try it. It doesn't have to be anything big. Have a "bring your lunch to work day" where everyone is encouraged to bring their own sack lunch. Sit with them and eat at the same table. Host a potluck or a pitch-in where everyone brings something to share with each other. Order pizza, have it delivered, and sit next to the employee who says the least. Watch them smile as you discuss life over pepperoni and cheese. Pass napkins and wipe your greasy mouth in their presence. Break bread with your team as often as you can – monthly, quarterly, or weekly if possible - to celebrate with care.

Caring Ways Enhance
the Circle of Life for Any Business

You may be thinking. . ."Look lady, I hired these associates. I owe them nothing more than that! They should be caring for me."

THEY DO CARE for you! They give you their time, sometimes much more of their time than is required or paid for by their wages. They give of their talent which is probably more valuable than the salary they make. On a job is where most people spend the majority of their time; this time is more than they spend with their own families or friends. It is good business to show the engaged employee that you care. They are responsible for caring for your customers. Period. It is what I call, the circle of life for any business – the manager takes care of the employee, the employee takes care of the customer, the customer takes care of the business by being a repeat customer, and the business will in-turn take care of the manager.

Well, it's up to you to continue the list of ways to care for your employees. Consider the ideas in this booklet your starter's kit for: creating an environment where employees can be happy, recognizing them as individuals, establishing trust, welcoming new hires, smiling at your team, being yourself, and taking time to dine with your staff. Hopefully, these ideas jump start you on your path to making a difference in the work lives of your team.

About the Author

MS. JOKIMA HILLER'S PASSION to please has helped her sustain an interesting career in the hospitality industry for over 20 years! Her blend of experience and education make her a great resource. She's held a variety of positions ranging from human resources clerk and assistant reservation sales manager to front office manager, regional trainer, and general manager. Her Bachelor's degree in Restaurant, Hotel, Institutional and Tourism Management from Purdue University – Calumet and Masters in Business Administration from Keller Graduate School of Management put her in positions to create best practices adopted by hotel colleagues, management, and franchise companies.

She is the co-author of the guide book, **The RevPAR Formula** that addresses ten of the top challenges for hotel managers and is a promoter of educating high school students about the hospitality industry via the online Hiller School of Hospitality.

She is currently an instructor at Missouri State University teaching courses in Hospitality Leadership, Lodging Management and Special Event Planning. She also specializes in online learning and social networking. She enjoys public speaking and has had numerous opportunities to facilitate work-shops on a variety of topics including keys to being a good leader in high school and meeting planner burnout.

**Visit www.hillerhospitality.com
for more information.**

Testimonials

Yolanda Carmin
General Manager at Best Western Plus
As Reported on LinkedIn®

"Jokima taught me how to be a better person all around. She always led by example. She strived to leave an impression on the entire staff and guests and did just that. Still almost a year after she has left this hotel her name is spoken in the greatest of admiration almost every day by both employees and guests."

November 14, 2008, Yolanda reported to Jokima at Country Inn & Suites at the Port

Gwen Hasse
General Manager at Nourish Restaurant

"Times are tough . . . for employers it's finding high quality staff who's salary fits into the budget. For employees, it's keeping the job (which used to be the job of 3 people) while maintaining credentials and a personal life. More than ever, employee recognition is essential for both parties. When your boss takes their time to find out your favorite soda, candy, and hand cream, etc. it shows that they care. We all know that gone are the days of significant pay raises but a little appreciation can go so much further. A happy employee means happy guests with results in ROI. This is a no brainer win/win!"

December 14, 2014, Gwen reported to Jokima at The Chef's Academy

Cecelia Jernegan
Author of Home Office Success 4 U
As Reported on LinkedIn®

"I opened several brick and mortar type businesses in the 70's and 80's and worked with hundreds of franchise business owners over the past 20 years. I can tell you what the great ones have in common: "Caring" about their employees who in turn take care of their customers. A great trait for any entrepreneur."

January 5, 2015, Cecelia worked with Jokima at Carlson Hotels Worldwide

Coni Wolk
District Director at Carlson Rezidor Hotel Group
As Reported on LinkedIn®

"Each shift begins by entering a "you" focused room. Snacks, beverages and inspirational messages surround the employees allowing them Ten Minutes of Happiness each day. This is only one example of Jokima's understanding of the value of the individual.

I have had the privilege of observing Jokima in many roles over the years. Her love of the Hospitality field comes in only second to her great passion for people. This shows in all aspects of her life whether it is in her teaching, mentoring, leading or simply in her relationships with her family and friends. She is unwavering in her pursuit to help others recognize and achieve their full potential; in doing so, she is fulfilling her own."

June 11, 2011, Coni worked with Jokima at Carlson Hotels Worldwide

Jill Woods
Regional Director Field Sales at Extended Stay Hotels

"I experienced firsthand Jokima's enthusiasm for employees and the difference it makes when they know you care. This guide is coming from an expert in bringing out the very best in employees even in the face of challenges. Her gift of knowledge and caring continues to influence many in the hospitality world and is transferable to other industries as well."

April 26, 2015, Jill reported to Jokima at the Country Inn & Suites, Indianapolis Airport South